Hair Clients for Life!

*Guide for Hairdressers to Connect
with and Retain Hair Clients for Life!*

Julie Holler

BALBOA.
PRESS

A DIVISION OF HAY HOUSE

Balboa Press books may be ordered through booksellers or by contacting:

Balboa Press
A Division of Hay House
1663 Liberty Drive
Bloomington, IN 47403
www.balboapress.com
1 (877) 407-4847

Because of the dynamic nature of the Internet, any web addresses or
links contained in this book may have changed since publication and
may no longer be valid. The views expressed in this work are solely those
of the author and do not necessarily reflect the views of the publisher,
and the publisher hereby disclaims any responsibility for them.

The author of this book does not dispense medical advice or prescribe
the use of any technique as a form of treatment for physical, emotional,
or medical problems without the advice of a physician, either directly
or indirectly. The intent of the author is only to offer information
of a general nature to help you in your quest for emotional and
spiritual well-being. In the event you use any of the information in
this book for yourself, which is your constitutional right, the author
and the publisher assume no responsibility for your actions.

Any people depicted in stock imagery provided by Thinkstock are
models, and such images are being used for illustrative purposes only.
Certain stock imagery © Thinkstock.

Print information available on the last page.

ISBN: 978-1-5043-6396-9 (sc)
ISBN: 978-1-5043-6397-6 (e)

Balboa Press rev. date: 10/21/2016

CONTENTS

INTRO

Hairdressing...

Why hairdressing? Why did you choose to become a hairdresser?

I hope your answer includes –" because I love my hands in hair, I'm creative, I like people, and I love designing the best looking & feeling hair I possibly can!" etc...

MOST important, I believe, is the desire to serve and help others to look and feel their best, while maintaining a great attitude and positive energy.

You, as a hairdresser, are working on people's HALO'S – CROWNING GLORY – a person's HAIR STYLE is one of the first things people notice about them...

What an important job you have to help the client you are servicing to look and feel terrific!

Did you know... that millions of people visit salons every day ... and that most choose their hairdresser mainly for psychological reasons... (Psychology Today). That tells me right there that they are in your chair for more reasons than just to get their hair cut...

You have a client in your chair for their very first visit with you... I am going to give you the communication skills and tips to connect with them and to KEEP them as your HAIR CLIENT FOR LIFE!

I want and hope this book becomes a tool, like your blow dryer, that you keep in your work station and refer to often... whether you are a stylist that is building a clientele, or a seasoned stylist looking to refresh and refuel. It will greatly improve the service you provide and the number of clients you continually service...

Review it. Pull it out any time you have a "slow day" or space in your day's schedule. Use it to refuel your motivation, give yourself a refresher if you are feeling burned out, and re-set your purpose as a hairdresser!

BIOGRAPHY

B.A. Communications/Journalism – Oakland University, Rochester, Michigan 1988

Public Relations Coordinator – 1989-1995

Cosmetology License – 1993-1995

Hairdresser – 1995-present

After completing college and working in the field of public relations for 5 years, I found myself with the desire to become a hairdresser. A hairdresser who was creative and helped others to look and feel their very best. I, myself, LOVED the feeling of a great hair day and wanted to create that same feeling on a regular basis for others.

The big question... Time and money aside... "What would YOU like to do in your work life if you could do anything?"

"BECOME A GREAT HAIRDRESSER??!!" Then this book WILL give you the interpersonal and communication skills to be one! You know, they say if you follow your heart... if you do what you love for your work – you'll never "work" a day in your life!

CLIENT'S 1ST VISIT

(consultation, the beginning of the relationship, the opportunity to give a great experience, shampoo service, hair focus, products/styling focus, 1 tip, products & prebook importance)

This appointment should always be booked with an extra 15 minutes since it is the client's 1st visit and extra time will be necessary.

Aaaaah, the first impression rule... Whenever you are greeting a client for the 1st time, the most important thing to do is to SMILE. Look into their eyes, and invite them to your station like you are welcoming someone that you are really looking forward to getting to know.

Get them seated and comfortable, and then ask them how they would like their hair to look. Let them answer... Let them lead... It's their hair, and their service time...

Responses will likely be:

"Just a cut" or "I want something new" or "I'm not sure" or they may know just what they want and show you pictures from their phone or a magazine… They may be in a hurry or they may have plenty of time. You'll be able to read this by the way they talk and act…

Let's say this 1st time client is booked with you for a haircut. Remember that this can be really nerve-wracking for a first-time client. They are willing to let you cut their hair, which has a big effect on how they look and feel. They are trusting that you will listen to how they would like it to look and that you will make them look great!

3 basic questions to ask each new hair cut client that sits in your styling chair:

1. Tell me about your hair – what do you like?
2. What don't you like about your hair?
3. How much time are you willing to spend each morning on your hair/styling it?

Discuss how the client would like their hair to look. Proceed and comment positively "Great, that will look terrific," or "Good choice, I know you'll love it".

To the shampoo bowl…

Whether you are shampooing your client or an assistant is shampooing your client, how many times have you heard, "Oh, this is my favorite part!"? Take note, and make sure to give TWO terrific shampoos and a conditioning… Shampoo thoroughly and with confidence. No wimpy scrubbing. Give their scalp a great massage. Ask about the water temperature. "Is it comfortable? Too warm? Too cool?"

Take this time, if you are doing the shampooing, to ask them about what shampoo and conditioner they use at home. Educate them. Also educate them on HOW to properly shampoo and condition their hair. So many clients have never been taught how much shampoo or conditioner to use for their hair, or how to properly cleanse and condition it. Let them know the importance of thoroughly wetting their hair, and pouring the right amount of shampoo for their hair type and length into their hands.

Let them know with an example such as "use the size of a quarter" and then instruct them to massage it well in to their scalp. Then to rinse well and gently blot excess water from their hair. Next, instruct them to pour the right amount of conditioner into their hands, again using an example such as "the size of a nickel" and to distribute throughout their ends and up the hair shaft, not touching the scalp, then to rinse. ALL clients will appreciate this education.

Many, especially all young girls with hair to their waist, pile their hair on top of their head and squirt the shampoo on and mush it around, barely cleansing the scalp and over cleansing their hair. They usually use way too much shampoo too. I always tell clients to gently massage their scalp with shampoo to cleanse, letting the water rinse the shampoo down the hair shaft for a gentle cleansing; and to condition their ends running the conditioner up the ends through their hair trying not to touch their scalp, then rinse.

Next, turban wrap a towel around their head so that they aren't dripping with water, and escort them back to your chair. (YouTube how to turban wrap if you don't already have this habit)

As you begin and proceed through their hair cut, chat about their HAIR. If they make small talk with you about the weather, the happenings of the day etc., that's fine; but redirect the conversation right back to THEIR HAIR.

Ask what they use to style it – what products do they like to use?

Ask how they usually wear their hair – down, pulled back, up, curled, straightened?

Ask how often they style it – every day, every other day, etc.?

When it's time to blow it dry, choose your styling products:

Show them what you are choosing,

Why you chose it, &

How much of the product you are putting into their hair.

For example, "I am going to use this (product name) in your hair to give you a smooth and conditioned finish today. This product is light weight, and won't be too heavy or weigh your hair down. It actually acts like a treatment once you apply heat to the hair from a blow dryer. I use this much (show the amount of product in your hands) for your hair type and length. I am running it all throughout your hair, through your ends, not touching your roots so as not to weigh your hair down."

"Next I am going to use this volumizing mousse. I am taking a golfball size (show) and working it into my hands, then I will massage it through this top "mohawk" section of your scalp. It will help to create lift and fullness off of your scalp, leaving smooth hair and ends thanks to the leave-in treatment."

Set both products in the middle of your counter, directly in front of the client and within arm's reach, and begin to blow dry.

Talk them through how you are blowdrying. (Talk lightly, let them relax and enjoy, but offer some education. WET- DAMP- DRY- SMOOTH – educate them on the importance of following through these 4 steps of getting the hair from wet to damp, damp to dry and dry to smooth for the best finish. Show them how to hold the brush... horizontal and up, perpendicular and back... etc. Show them, have them watch in the mirror. Especially when you are styling the front – bangs, fringe, top for lift or smoothness...

Say "HERE'S A TIP..." and only say this once during their first visit. Offer a simple tip about styling and finishing their hair. They'll remember it and you won't overwhelm them trying to teach them all of your techniques in one visit... save more for the next visits to come...

After the blow dry, finish with a flat iron, curling wand or other tool of your choice and show them how you are using it too – proper temperature, heat protect spray and how to use it, how long to hold the tool in place or how to glide a flat iron. Again, a light education...

Finish! Hair spray, gloss spray, paste, etc. and instruct.

Mirror – hand your client a hand mirror to view how great their hair looks in the back too!

Now, ask how they FEEL.

"How do you feel? Do you like it? Are you comfortable with it? Any questions?" Often you will hear, "I LOVE IT!" "I JUST WISH I COULD GET IT TO LOOK LIKE THIS!" Your response? "No problem! You can! And I'll teach you!" (Next visit...) "The next time I get to see you, I'll work with you again. There's an art to styling hair and your hair is awesome! You'll learn it!" ... always give a positive response and give them the feeling that with a bit of practice – they can do it!

Front Desk – escort your new client to the front desk for check-out.

Products – ask if they would like to take the products that you used to style their hair today home with them.

Close of visit & Pre-book importance – "Thank you (and say their name). It was great meeting you. I loved doing your hair today!" Make sure their cell phone number and email address have been entered into the salon's system and make note for your personal system of client notes. Leave them not only with that awesome feeling you get when you just love your hair, but now they also feel that you genuinely liked meeting them and getting the opportunity to help them look and feel great!

Imagine... leaving a doctor's office for the 1st time... The doctor shakes your hand, smiles and looks right at you saying, "Thank you. It was great meeting you and getting the opportunity to help you feel better." (WOW -- I'm going back again!!)

Offer to pre-book their next appointment so that they can return on the day and time that works best for them. With a scheduled appointment, you have the opportunity to give them another great experience that they will definitely come back and look forward to! Oh, and so that you can share more styling tips!

CLIENT'S 2ND VISIT

(consultation, creating the relationship, offering another great experience, hair focus, pictures, products & pre-book importance)

They're back! You're so happy to see them!

"Hi (name)! Come on over to my station. Tell me how your hair is working for you. What worked? What didn't work?" Let your client talk...

Then add "What can I do today to help you love it even more?"

Discuss...

Refresh their goals with their hair... Consult again!

What do they want?

Q. Dimension? (color)

Q. Shine? (color, products, styling)

Q. Strength? (products)

Q. Softness? (products, styling)

Q. Warmth? Cooler in tone? (color)

Q. Ease? (cut, color, styling, products)

Q. Texture? (cut, texturizing service, products)

Q. Certain look? (from a picture, etc.)

What challenges do they have?

Flat/dry?

Frizzy/curly?

Gray?

Too warm/brassy tone?

Too cool/ashy tone?

Thin/fine?

Too dark in color?

Too blonde in color?

Weight/layers?

Bangs/fringe?

Color fading?

Doesn't know how to style/Old styling habits?

There are solutions to all of these... Begin with their wants and challenges...and the desired look. Then offer your solution.

WORDAGE – it's so important...

"Now, here's my goal for your hair..." Explain & give benefits:

As an example, you are offering 'controlled damage' by adding highlights which will add body to their hair by opening up the cuticle of the hair shaft and expanding it to make their hair feel more full.

If it's a color correction or you're taking their hair in a new direction, let them know – "We might nail it this time, or it may take me until the 2nd opportunity to get your color balanced and just the way you'd like it to look because..." (and explain why).

This sets your client up to feel that you know what you're doing, that you have a plan, are giving them realistic expectations and can get them to their goal.

PICTURES

When your client shows you a picture of what they like/ how they want their hair to look...

STOP...

Don't think... ok, that's a level 5 base with some highlights... Take a moment to ask, "What do you like about this look in the picture?" They may respond with "the highlights" or "the layers"... if their answer is "the color", hold the picture (on their phone or from the magazine) up alongside their face. Give them a hand mirror to see up close and make sure that they still like that color ON THEM. Do they have the same skin tone as the model in the picture? Is the color too dark?

I do this with pictures brought in by my clients and so often their comment, once they hold it up close to their own face, is "oooooh, that's too dark," or "yah, but maybe not that red." Red?! They see red in a warm lowlight color. Look closely at Jennifer Aniston's color, which is likely one of the most often requested blonde hair colors, and there are several shades of caramel and sometimes strawberry running through her base color. Often it is the lighting in which the photograph is taken, so also take that into effect when holding it up near your client's cheek or jawbone to get a feel if the color is right for them.

This will avoid a color gone wrong. A few extra moments of detective work will save you altering it and not only build your credibility, which shows that you sure know what you're talking about when it comes to hair color and what looks best on them, but also your client will feel comfortable and love their results.

One last suggestion, when a client is requesting a darker color than what they are currently wearing, or wants to go from blonde to brunette... (You know how hard it is to go dark, decide it's too dark, and then go lighter... the hair suffers and it's time consuming...) My answer is always – "Let's move in that direction and take your hair color darker in stages. It will be better for the integrity of your hair and also will give you and your hair time to adjust to the change." Select a shade that isn't quite as dark as the picture they are showing. Or if they are going from blonde to brunette, weave out some face framing highlights so that there is still a hint of brightness around their face. This is a great technique to do when taking a client's color darker.

Pictures are great to work from. But those are the key words... TO WORK FROM.

Again, so often the color appears the way it looks in the picture due to the lighting... explain this to your client. Or the model in the picture has extensions put in for the photo to provide that fullness and length... explain that and the options there... Or their hair is professionally curled and styled and given a textured or beach wave finish with styling products and tools – then the model's head is tousled and 'click' the photograph is taken. Tough look to achieve and maintain with just a perm... However, if that is the look they like and that they want to achieve, educate them on their options:

A perm with styling education, products and tools...

OR, just styling education with the right cut, products and tools (depending on their hair type).

The END RESULT can be similar depending on their hair, its condition, etc...

Show them – Educate them.

Show them how to curl it. OR, perm it and show them what to do when styling their hair to help it look like the photo.

EDUCATE – EDUCATE – I can't tell you how much this will set you apart from other hairdressers and how it will gain you such appreciation from your client. I know you're busy and crunched for time, but a few extra minutes used to EDUCATE by showing them and walking them through HOW TO FINISH THEIR HAIR will set you apart from a hairdresser who chats their way through the finishing phase of their client's hair. Their hair may look fantastic, but the client will feel frustrated at home when they go to style it ... what product ? how much to use? how to style and finish it? Etc...

Back to the art of the consultation –

Ask Questions,

Listen,

Offer Solutions and Educate,

From Start to Finish.

Now, the front desk check out...

Close and give the opportunity to take products home with them that you used in their hair today.

Offer to pre-book their next appointment -- It's essential. You are wrapping up their 2nd visit. If you get a response like, "I'll call – need to check my planner..." Answer with "Let's get you a slot in my schedule and if you need to change it – no worries – just call."

CLIENT'S 3RD VISIT

(consultation, client focus, hair goals, hair stories, relationship building, essential client questions to know, products & pre-book importance)

Back again!

SO glad to see them!

Get them comfortable in your chair, "Tell me, how is your hair working for you?"

Go over their hair goals:

Length

Layers/Weight

Fringe/Bangs

Color/Texture/Condition

A Great Question to ask: "(Say their name...), whose hair do you wish yours could look like the most?"

OR, "With your own hair, what quality do you wish it had the most?..." More smooth?, more shine?, less frizz?, not so flat?, easier to blow-out?, NOW – with their answer, OFFER A SOLUTION!

Let's talk CLIENT FOCUS... Who doesn't like to feel that they are being listened to, cared for and serviced well? Focus on your client while they are there in the salon with you. Talk HAIR first, then you can chat and be social on other topics. If they are going to be sitting in another area of the salon while their hair service is processing, tend to them with a quick check-in:

"Are you comfortable?"

"Are you ready for something to drink?"

Let them know, "Your color is coming along great" – peek in at a foil or check how their base color is processing... Let them know the approximate processing time to go – never put a timer near them – keep it with you – on your station, etc. You are in control of their processing time...

When your client is in your chair, your FOCUS is on them. A client can be in your care for ½ hour to 3 hours... sometimes longer, depending on the services they are receiving from you... Always visit and chat in a POSITIVE WAY. If they get going on a negative topic, redirect them and talk about something related to their hair... or at least a positive subject. Talking about negative things or topics will leave them feeling deflated (not to mention, you too!). Talking about positive things and topics will help them to feel good and refreshed when they leave their visit with you!

I CAN'T EMPHASIZE THIS ENOUGH.

Get 100% clear about 100% focus on your client,

AND KEEP IT POSITIVE.

Focus on their life, their events, THEIR HAIR. When they ask about you, your life, your kids, etc … give a positive response, but keep it BRIEF, share but redirect the conversation right back to focusing on THEM.

Also, always find a way to talk about PRODUCTS during your service time with your client. We KNOW what a difference products can make for our own hair. "Remind me, what are you shampooing and conditioning with at home in the shower?" OK if a professional product is used that is best for their hair, or RECOMMEND what they should be using and WHY.

You'd be surprised how many clients say "I don't use conditioner, it makes my hair feel too heavy." WHAT!? They have likely chosen the wrong conditioner in the past. Educate them on why a conditioner is essential, especially if they have color treated hair. It provides much-needed moisture and detangles.

"So what's on your bathroom counter at home that you reach for when you go to style your hair?" TEACH… styling products, their benefits and how much to use, and how to apply. Touch on tools and what and how to use.

Use stories... old blow dryer, old hot rollers, wrong brush, flat iron temperature setting, etc... Explain how important it is to be using proper tools to style and finish their hair.

An Example STORY: I tell about my client whose hair looked so "fried" in the back of her head. I had been doing her hair for several years and when I saw her for a visit and was trying to determine why her hair was looking so "fried" in the middle back section of her hair, she said "it must be the color and we need to do something!" Well, as I explained to her, the permanent color I use on her hair only touches her new-growth area... glossing touches her ends which would condition, not FRY her hair. As I asked her more questions, "tell me, how do you style your hair? ...walk me through your process..." (I was thinking flat iron or curling iron damage... especially with it occurring on her ends...). She replied that she had been setting her hair with hot rollers. Ah, just how old were those hot rollers? Well, she'd had them forever. So long that with further questioning, she admitted that they felt like they were burning her scalp when she placed them in. Any heat protectant used? (Nope.) How was the surface of the hot rollers? Had the protective coating on the roller worn off? (Yep.) Sometimes we get to be hair detectives!

Another Example STORY to share involved the same situation but with a client's bangs. She too thought it must be the color I was using that was frying her hair in the front... I explained that it couldn't be the color, because again, I don't run permanent color past the new growth area that I am covering. That hair must be mechanically damaged... so I asked questions about her styling routine... Come to find out, her "favorite brush" that she had for decades to round brush her bangs, was so worn out that it was frying her hair when she held the blow dryer up to it. All of the protective coating on the round base of the brush had worn off. Another opportunity to check in with your client about proper tools, their longevity, and how to properly use a brush and dryer. My client was also holding the blow dryer right on the brush, for too long without any movement... fried bangs was no surprise!

So shut off your mind buzz, dial it to OFF...

Focus and give your full attention to your client and their hair during the visit. If you're thinking about something or someone else – hit PAUSE in your head – you can revisit it later... right now, you are giving 100% to your client. And trust me, they feel it.

WHY DO CLIENTS LEAVE THEIR STYLISTS?

When asked, it's because they didn't feel appreciated or listened to, or wanted something new and it wasn't offered.

ARE YOU OFFERING THIS ATTENTION EACH AND EVERY VISIT?

WHY WOULD A FRIEND OR PARTNER LEAVE A RELATIONSHIP??

Hmmmm... could be the same reasons. We've all heard that it takes consistent work and time and attention for anything that is worthwhile. It is not only important to keep yourself educated and informed of techniques, but even more important to work on your relationships with your clients. On a regular basis. Never take them for granted. Never pre-mix their color because you know that she will be walking through the door on the first Tuesday of the month at 4pm. They are a committed relationship to you if they become a regular "Hair Client for Life". Treat them with the appreciation they deserve. Greet them each time they arrive for their appointment like you are so happy to see them! Get them comfortable and always consult. Every visit. No exception. "How is your hair working? Any challenges?"

"How would you love it to look today?"

And then LISTEN...

There is always something new and fresh to talk about in hairdressing. A new product, a new service, treatment, different way to style their hair, a new trend, what you are seeing in hair on the streets and in your community... Ask them how THEIR friends are wearing their hair these days...

Again, if you are at a lull in the conversation, TALK HAIR. YOU, as a stylist, know A LOT MORE than your client does about all that goes into making their hair look great. Share your knowledge – you'll get a reaction like, "Wow, no one ever told me how to smooth my hair out before", or "Wow, no one ever took the time to really show me how to style my bangs"... and you know what that means, your client will tell their friends! Especially as they start getting compliments on their hair because it looks so great every day, and that is because THEIR

HAIRDRESSER actually educated them on HOW to style their hair to make it look great every day!

AND GUYS ... not all guys know how to apply product in their hair to get it to look great! Show them. Show them when to apply it (wet, damp or dry), how much, and HOW to apply the product...

THEY DON'T KNOW

WHAT YOU KNOW

YOU'RE AN EXPERT

SHOW OFF YOUR KNOWLEDGE

YOUR CLIENT WILL BENEFIT!

Especially when you're tailoring it to their hair!

So, during the finishing process, talk about the products you are choosing to finish their hair, why you are choosing those products and what benefits they have for their hair type. Show how much you are using of each product and how to apply it in their hair. Be specific, give examples, then place the products in their lap or right in front of them on your counter.

Next proceed to style, letting them know how you are holding the dryer, brush, how far from their head, etc. Let them know how much time to expect it will take them to blow their hair out properly. Show them how to section it to gain more control of their hair. Most will rush through the drying phase, stopping before it's smooth. WET – to DAMP – to DRY – to SMOOTH. Don't skip the SMOOTHING step. I tell my clients to look at the time and add an extra few minutes to completely go through their hair one last time with their blow dryer and brush, to thoroughly smooth and lock in their blow out. It's another tip that clients will just love. "I always remember what you told me... I'm not done when my hair feels dry," my client Diana says. "I need to spend an extra 5 minutes with my round brush and blow dryer to really get it to that smooth finish. It makes all the difference!"

Remember tool choice too. Ask your client what type of blow dryer, brush, and styling tools they have and use at home. Recommend and offer if they need to replace or update. Your clients will love you for these tips, and it's part of the relationship building process. Just like sharing something you know with a friend...

And don't forget your male clients. Their styles and trends are changing just as often, if not more so, than for women. Watch trends, take male cutting and styling and product knowledge classes; and as we know today, so much can be learned with education on the Internet. Stay current and be the first to show your male clients where their side burns should hit, how to style their hair a different way to create a different finish. Introduce them to the latest product trend for men. If they are wearing gel in their hair today, show them what affect a hair paste or pomade will do.

I have showed so many of my male clients just how to apply finishing product in their hair... I've taught them that most often, for mens styles, their hands are their best tools. Show them how much product to use, how to distribute it into their hands and fingers, and just how to run it through their hair to finish their look – this isn't natural for all men, so instructing them is so appreciated.

WHAT YOU MUST KNOW ABOUT EACH AND EVERY ONE OF YOUR CLIENTS:

These questions are great to ask clients when cutting or styling their hair... or when you are cutting their hair and are struggling for conversation... (Yet you are likely never to struggle for conversation with any client, ever again, now that you know how to talk about hair related topics that will surely benefit that client!)

ASK:

1. WHAT they shampoo and condition with at home & HOW they shampoo and condition their hair...

Make sure to recommend the right shampoo and conditioner for their hair, the benefits of using professional shampoo and conditioner, and how to properly cleanse and condition their hair type.

2. HOW they "towel dry" their hair...

Yikes!, make sure they don't roughen up their hair with the towel and rub it too harshly, which is sure to promote breakage and cause frizz and damage. Most clients don't know that hair is much more fragile and prone to breakage when wet. Educate them on how to gently blot excess water from their hair with a towel to remove water weight without roughening up the cuticle of their hair shaft.

3. HOW they comb or brush through their hair when it's wet or damp...

Instruct them to use a wide tooth comb or vent brush, moving through their ends from bottom to top for long hair so as not to tug or break.

4. WHAT product they apply to their hair before blow drying and styling and HOW MUCH product...

What products are they reaching for before they blow dry? (So many times when I've asked this question, the response is "nothing!"... Yikes. Educate them on the importance of using a finishing product to protect, enhance, and hold their style).

Educate them on what leave-in products are best for their hair type and show them how much product to use, giving an example that is easy to remember such as "size of a nickel".

5. WHAT finishing tools they use...

What do they use to style with? A blow dryer, then flat iron, curling iron, etc. Ask about what tools they have at home and how long they have had them. Share with them how important it is to replace and upgrade if needed.

Educate on proper heat settings and techniques. Also the importance of using a heat protect product in their hair.

6. HOW do they approach styling their hair...

Ask how they blow dry and style their hair and give them suggestions, especially as you are blow drying and styling their hair.

7. HOW MUCH TIME do they have to dry, style and finish their hair – 5 or 25 mins?

This will impact how they style and finish their hair, and if they only have a small amount of time, offer them ideas and solutions.

8. HOW OFTEN they wash their hair...

Give recommendations regarding their hair type and educate on products available that are good for every day washing as well as dry shampoo products and how to apply dry shampoo correctly which will extend a great blow dry.

9. DO they have tricks or techniques for 2nd or 3rd day hair?

Show them great ways to wear 2nd or 3rd day hair that are quick and easy. Also talk about the benefits of using a dry shampoo or an oil on their ends if their hair would benefit. I have shown many of my female clients how to re-activate product in their hair on day 2 or 3, and how to re-vamp their style with the heat of their blow dryer and a brush for another great hair day in minutes!

10. Their occupation & HOW they like their hair to look and feel...

Share your tips, your tricks, and offer them suggestions and ideas.

KEEP YOUR FIRST 3 VISITS geared toward hair talk and education... not sales... but talk and education... trust me, the sales will come from your talk and education naturally.

Now you know the drill... Pre-book their next appointment, and ask if they would like to take the products that you used for their hair today home with them.

CLIENT'S 4TH VISIT

(consultation, stylist/client relationship, offering change, client focus, positive talk, styling lesson, talk/teach/perform, products & pre-book importance)

Now they are really liking you. They are back for their 4th visit with you. Greet them like a new, yet comfortable friend. You are so happy to see them! First impressions rule... every time... not just the first visit. This is your client that you are servicing. A client that has chosen you and that you would like to keep for life!

I always compliment my client as soon as I see them... It can be hair-related or something else personal that is a positive compliment. "You look fabulous!" or "You look fantastic! Were you just on vacation!?" Find a way to lift them up before they even sit down in your styling chair... "Cute bag! – Great fashion sense you have!" or "Cool boots! You always look so trendy!" With your male clients as well, it's just as important... Find something specific you can compliment on, a detail. It starts the visit off on the up-swing. You never know... that client may not hear a nice compliment again until their next hair appointment with you! And you are in the "feel good" business... compliments FEEL good.

If you really stop to think for a moment, once you've had a client return to visit you for 6 visits... wouldn't you consider them "your client"? And if you had all returning clients, you wouldn't have to work so hard to get or attract "new clients". You could pre-book most of "your clients" that consistently schedule their hair appointments with you... leaving you a day of familiar faces, familiar hair (no guess work of underlying color or total overhauls!), and the opportunity to service your clients throughout their lives and many hair needs...

Keep this 4th visit like the 3rd... Personal to their hair needs, educational, offer color options, seasonal, conditioning, texture options, etc... With an existing client you can get to know them, their hair, offer them change on a regular basis and begin to build a real stylist/client relationship.

Talk TRENDS... CHANGE you are seeing – on the streets, in your trade publications, classes, on celebrities, the run-way, or tailor what "you're seeing" to their community of people; for example – moms, athletes, college kids, fashion-minded women, business men, -- discuss what the influences are (clean, edgy, boho chic, 70's inspired cuts, etc.).

Offer a styling lesson at their next visit if they are struggling with their blow-outs /finishes.

Talk products again...

Discuss easy ways to "soften" their blonde hair color or take them from a warm season into a cooler season by deepening their color without losing their blonde identity. For example, "Now that fall is here, let's talk about adding soft blonde highlights around your face and adding some caramel lowlights throughout the sides and the back of your hair to transition your hair color into Fall (always add a yummy name for the color – "caramel, warm chocolate, buttery", etc...).

Blonde hair color has so much dimension these days. Don't get stuck in a rut of just highlighting with the same lightener... Add some other blonde hues to your bowl and change up your pattern of highlighting. Keep it interesting and tell them when you are changing up the colors and patterns and why... Another reason they will get really attached to your skills for their hair...

Focus on Trends – Change – Styling Tips – Product Knowledge – Options now or down the road for their color, texture, cut/length... Have a "plan" for their hair... it will keep them interested, ready for change, and feeling like you are on it, with it, thinking about them for what's coming up next...

Also at this visit, start to chat about other topics to broaden your connection with them, but VERY IMPORTANTLY focus your chat on THEM – their work, their kids, their pets, their partner, their home, their day, ... when they ask about you, respond positively ALWAYS. Keep your troubles and personal negatives to yourself. Only share positive things to discuss, which keeps your client's visit feeling positive. Chat a minute or two with your response to their questions about you personally, then direct the conversation RIGHT back to them.

Always offer support, positive feedback, uplifting comments and praise.

WORTH SAYING AGAIN: Always offer support, positive feedback, uplifting comments and praise.

This is their time, not an opportunity to talk and work out your "stuff"... that's for your own off time to discuss with your family and friends. Many hairdressers use their time during the day with their clients to discuss their own stuff and work out their own issues... it's not your hair therapy time... it's your client's... They need to feel listened to and uplifted each and every hair visit. If you provide this, along with great hair service, your clients will be yours for life!

I'm sure you've heard clients say, "I always feel so good when I leave your salon!" A. You have worked on their HALO and B. You have listened to them. You don't have to solve their problems or even offer advice or suggestions... just listen, and respond so that they know they are heard. Besides a therapist, what other service provider truly listens, or has the opportunity to listen for more than 5-10 minutes? We are POSITIVE SERVICE PROVIDERS... And we are really lucky to get to provide a positive service.

MORE COMPLIMENTS!

Be Sincere...

"I love...!" As you are blow drying their hair, try saying, "I love this! Your hair looks great!" "You have the best hair!" or "Your hair is perfect for this cut!" Or "Get ready to turn heads today!" Or "Your cuteness factor just went WAY up!" (this is a favorite of my older female clients).

If your client answers with "I wish you could come over every morning and style it for me!" or "It looks good when you style it!" or "I just wish I could get it to look this good!"...

Opportunity -- Let them know that you offer STYLING LESSONS!

"I'm going to schedule a styling lesson for you! I will teach you how to blow your hair out so you can learn all the techniques and tricks that I know to get your hair looking amazing every day!" Book a 1 hour appointment for them. Walk them through the shampoo, conditioning, styling product choices and the amount and application of the styling products. Have them apply the styling products so that they get a feel as to how much to apply and how to apply them in their hair. You teach – they do the work. It's the best way for them to remember...

Next walk them through the step-by-step blow dry process. Because, again, if they do it they'll remember how to do it. Charge by the hour... It will take an hour to go through the process thoroughly. And it is a process... They may say, "I don't have this much time in the morning!" Ok, but as you know, anything you practice, you get better at doing and faster at doing... Reinforce that with practice, they will get it done much faster, just as you do.

You weren't a blow-dry master right out of beauty school! Let them know that by even applying 2 techniques that they learn today and building on them, it will make a difference in how their hair feels and looks!

As they are blow drying, show them how to section their hair so that they can gain control of the amount of hair to dry in each section. Show them how to hold the blow dryer and brush – really pay attention – watch – help them make adjustments – they are doing the work, yet you need to guide them step-by-step. With detail. Once they experience the process from putting the products into their hair, to drying and finishing their hair, they will retain and remember it because they went through the steps from start to finish.

Stick with them. Pay attention to every detail of their styling efforts. Be very present. And charge accordingly. Recap and have them write down or note in their phone the steps they took to achieve their finished look. This way they can refer to it when they are at home styling their hair.

During any service portion of your client's hair visits:

TALK – positive, supportive and about THEM…

TEACH – educate on products, tools, techniques, and what to use…

PERFORM – while styling, talk about & teach HOW to style their hair…

Now pre-book their next visit and always always always (should be a habit with every client now) ask if they would like to take the products that you used in their hair today HOME WITH THEM.

CLIENT'S 5TH VISIT

(consultation, connect, experience, compliments, gratitude, uplift, products & pre-book)

Initial greeting – Huge Smile. Greet your client with warmth and enthusiasm... Pretend you are opening up the front door of your home to see your good friend that you haven't seen in a month!

Consult – Always... Every single time... Get your client seated in your styling chair in front of the mirror before you whisk them back to the shampoo bowl or color application area... Take a good look at their hair. Ask what their wants/goals are for how they want their hair to look today... How is it feeling, working, styling, looking... EVERY time. Sit...connect for a moment...then proceed...

People leave their routines and come to YOU. Make them FEEL special. Once you give them an experience, they will never forget it and will want to return for that same FEELING.

People will pay, not only for great hair, but to change their state of mind and how they are feeling. How many times has a client arrived with a headache and upon leaving their visit – it's gone! Or they arrive feeling ok, and leave walking on air because their hair looks so great and you have made them feel special!

Create an experience for your client while they are in your care getting their hair done. It will set you worlds apart from other hairdressers.

FOCUS... FOCUS... FOCUS

Ask about THEM. Remove your "self" and "mind chatter" and put it on a shelf or in your drawer...whatever habit works best for you. Promise to do this and focus on your client. You can get back to your own stuff after your work day. You'll do yourself a favor too. Focusing on others sure helps to lighten your own thought load.

"Good Morning Beautiful!"

"Hello Handsome!"

Open your heart and your energy toward your client as a person FIRST, next focus in on their HAIR. This takes only a moment, and your client feels it.

At the end of your day with your clients, I promise that before you pick up your "self thoughts" again, you will count your blessings, realize that your own issues, struggles and what ever you were stressing about that morning, may be very small compared to another's struggle...

Count your blessings at the end of each day serving your clients... Become a part of the whole GRATITUDE MOVEMENT. What you give thanks for, multiplies... Give thanks for the opportunity to service your clients, each and every day... Make it a habit. And watch your client list GROW!

As a hairdresser, you're a giver. You're really working on their HALO. Look for a way to lift your client up while they are with you. Every visit. Even in a small way. That's enough.

Now do what you do best. Give them another terrific hair service so that they feel fantastic.

Up to the front desk to offer products and pre-book.

They will be back!

CLIENT'S 6TH VISIT

("your" client, connect, be their source, refresher education/tips, "dusting", make them feel special, staying fresh and current, offering change, offering products every time & pre-book)

You've won them as a client!

NOW KEEP them!

Greet them like you are so happy to see them, each and every time. Not only because they are a portion of your paycheck; but because by now, you are developing a relationship with them in hopes to nurture it for many years to come.

"What shall we do to spice up your hair this visit?!" Is one opener for this appointment.

"How are you feeling about your hair?" Get your client to tell you how they are FEELING...about their hair.

Offer ideas, suggestions, extra services to meet their hair needs...

As you've serviced your client over the course of their last 5 visits, make sure you are keeping detailed notes and recording formulas for their color and texture services. Note personal information, such as their spouse's name and kids' names... Promise yourself that you won't take your client for granted. Now that you've put in the extra effort to retain them, it is a lot easier to keep them as a client than to start from scratch trying to advertise for new clients or attract walk-ins.

Your appointment book can always be full once you've won over your clients and they pre-book and schedule with you. Now your books are filled with great clients that you enjoy and you know what to expect. Your income is consistent. Everything flows beautifully.

Gather each and every client's e-mail address and cell phone number. Send them notes and thoughts with pictures and ideas regarding their hair. It will endure them to you.

EXAMPLES...

(text or e-mail them...)

Hope you're having a GREAT hair day!

Thinking of you - how did your hair work for you on your vacation?!

How did your up-do hold up all night? Send me a picture!

Ok... how many hair compliments today?! (after a recent change)

(With picture) Check out (morning news personality or actress) – her cut and style would look amazing on you!

TRENDS – WHAT'S IN – BE THE SOURCE – BE THEIR HAIR SOURCE!

Draw – match – tailor trends to their hair... Suggest!

EVERY TIME your client sits down in your chair... before they are shampooed, take 2 minutes to take a look at their hair – dry and styled – and ask them, "HOW is your hair working for you?"

Zip your lips and listen... Let them answer.

Then, let them know you have suggestions.

Always Consult... Really take a good look at their hair. Is the hair spray they are using giving their hair a really dry appearance? Are they needing styling help?

EXAMPLE: ask what hair spray they've been using. If the response is, "I ran out of the stuff you had me using so I just picked up a bottle at the grocery store" (ugh...). Explain how drying the grocery store brand products can be on their hair and make sure that they leave with 2 bottles of the best professional hair spray product for their hair type THIS VISIT!

Always Offer Solutions,

Always Listen,

STOP and LOOK – proceed with their service.

Getting their hair shampooed is something that your regular clients will always look forward too... As a reminder, ALWAYS give your client 2 thorough shampoos, massaging and invigorating their scalp, followed by a conditioning.

NEVER RUSH... NO MATTER WHAT. They will feel it.

It calms and relaxes them... You too.

If you have an assistant, often say, "Please make sure to give (client's first name) a terrific shampoo and conditioning today – she's worth it!" Or... "he deserves it!"...

Remember, the shampoo service is the best time to ask them what they are using at home to cleanse and condition, and it is also a great time to teach them proper cleansing and conditioning techniques. Your clients will sure appreciate the education. Their expensive bottle of shampoo or tub of conditioner doesn't come with tailored directions just for THEIR hair...

Then when it's time to style their hair... stop your chatting on whatever positive topic you are discussing and say, "Ok, your hair... Remind me what you're putting in your hair before you blow it dry."

Next, ask "HOW are you applying your product?" Even if you've gone over this with them before... Ask. We can breeze through their hair with our product of choice, working it into the scalp or slipping it through the ends of their hair. It's effortless because we are knowledgeable with the products we choose and we use them all day long. SO often I have asked a client to show me how they are applying a product... They are usually not using enough, or they are using way too much and are applying it all wrong! It isn't instinctual for clients to know how to apply a root boosting spray or just how to apply a smoothing leave-in treatment. And for young men who are just starting to use product in their hair, they don't know what to do with that product that looks like cement in a hockey puck!

Hand your client the product from your station, talk them through just how much to put in to their hands (size of a pea...size of a quarter...).

Next remind them about HOW to apply it into their hair. Show them with your hands (since they have the product in their hands) and have them do it right after you've shown them. This way they will remember and also know just the right amount of product to use.

If they do it, they'll remember it. (Have a damp towel to wipe their hands on after they've distributed the products into their hair.)

Now they are comfortable and relaxed. Go ahead and proceed with their blow out. Talk them through the mechanics of their blow out as a "refresher"... not too technical but including a few tips for them to remember.

(Such as how to section the hair for blowing dry or how to really smooth out their fringe/bang area).

If time allows, show them proper hand placement with the brush, blow-dryer placement with nozzle, blowing downward on the cuticle of the hair shaft... slow to the ends... drying – smoooooothing.

Flat iron use (temperature for their hair type, heat protect spray, sectioning, glide, etc.).

Curling iron/wand use (temperature, heat protect spray, sectioning, techniques, etc.).

You can't have your day running behind, but just showing one styling technique or bit of education will again endure them to you and your care for their hair.

If you haven't already, this might be the time to offer a styling lesson appointment. You can focus all of your attention on their style and have them do the start to finish work so they can commit it to memory!

Schedule that 1 hour styling lesson. Set your price by the hour. They will love you for it! From the shampoo bowl, where you remind them the proper way to shampoo their scalp and condition their hair with the right products for their hair type, back to your chair where they do the mechanics and you are their guide.

6 months down the road, schedule another styling appointment, if needed, to build on their "tool box of hair tricks".

Trust me, your clients will tell their friends that THEIR hairdresser TAUGHT them how to finish their hair...

Get ready for a long list of their friends as new clients!!

There is a lot more to good hair dressing than great technical skills...

COMMUNICATION & LISTENING SKILLS are KEY. Open the conversation and LISTEN...

Get the client's feelings about their hair – hands in their hair – eyes on their hair...

Always ask, "How did you like your last hair cut?"

"Was it easy to manage?"

"Anything giving you trouble?"

If the client ever needs a freshening up but doesn't want a "hair cut" because they are afraid you'll take too much off or cut it too short ...

Offer a "dusting"... This term became popular with several of my clients who had fine/thin hair. They would come regularly for color services but didn't want a "hair cut" with each visit, so I would "dust it" just to clean up the ends and fringe area. Show your client that they will hardly find any hair on the floor from your "dusting", yet their hair will be easier to manage and will look refreshed. Thickens up their ends too. Men like a dusting if they aren't due for a regular hair cut but have an important date in between – work or otherwise. (Price your "dusting" accordingly).

Remember to EDUCATE your YOUNG CLIENTS:

Young, long-haired clients – show them how to shampoo their scalp, how much shampoo to use, and how to condition their ends. "Shampoo your scalp to cleanse. Rinse well. Condition your ends, moving from the tips up the hair shaft without touching your scalp, then rinse." All of my young clients with long hair know this tip.

I have a young client that has such thick hair, especially in the back of her head at the nape area. I could tell that she wasn't cleansing her hair well, likely she was pouring the shampoo on top of her head and sudsing up on top. I told her that when she shampoos her hair from now on, to place the shampoo in her hands, size of a quarter, and to bend her head forward in the shower. Next; to place the shampoo right at the nape of her neck and move it up toward the top of her head, almost like she were washing her hair in a stand up sink. I told her to concentrate on the underneath portion of her hair first, then to gently lift her head back upright and rinse. This will help her to cleanse where her hair is most thick and right at her scalp (which is what needs cleansing). The rinsing will gently cleanse her ends. She called me to tell me what a difference it made and how much better her hair feels!

Young boys and young men – show them how much shampoo to use and how to use products in their hair to create different effects. Also the amount of product to use. Have THEM put the product in their hair. It will help them to remember how to do it. They will love you for it! Make them feel super comfortable.

I had a young boy that really liked the style that stuck up in the front and kicked forward over his forehead. I showed him what product to use and how to apply it to get his front to "kick". He decided that his bangs looked like a cross between a jump and a ramp... so we nick-named his signature look "the jamp" hair cut! He came in for 2 years straight asking for the "jamp cut." Now he's moved on to a different look, but it was fun for him and it made him feel special!

THINGS TO KEEP YOU FRESH:

Magazines & catalogues (breeze through even your junk mail, just to get a look at how the models are wearing their hair in the pictures),

Television (watch for hair trends and styles - on a variety of channels and networks),

Internet sites (Google hair style trends and take note on social media),

The vibe on the streets where you live,

The vibe and look on the streets elsewhere. Whenever you travel, take note of how the people in that community or city are wearing their hair. Whenever I have a client traveling to a different region of the country or overseas, I ask them to notice how people are wearing their hair and to report back to me! It's a fun assignment, gets them thinking of you on their trip as well as how others in different parts of our world are wearing their hair!

CHANGE:

Offer to make their hair look spring-ready and sun-kissed! Even if they aren't going to Hawaii... Suggest "Let's make you look like you've just been to the islands!"

Offer to make their hair look conditioned and richly toned for Fall...

Offer change... even a small subtle one. Your client may not choose to make a change to their hair this visit, but they will love that you are offering. You are the director... And your client will know that they will never be in a hair rut with you in charge!

In fact, never let your scheduled appointments dictate what you will do with your client's hair. If your client is scheduled in for a highlight and a trim, don't just highlight their hair color. Look at it first. What does it need? What would make it look more interesting? More rich? You're creative! Get your creative mindset working – it's so much more rewarding and fun. And your clients will love love love you for it!

You've won this client over. 6 visits. Fantastic!

Now escort them up to your front desk, schedule in their next appointment, offer the products that you used in their hair today to take home – every time. They may pass on products today, but won't pass every time. And remember, your goal isn't necessarily to push products, it's to make sure that they have everything they need to re-create the same great look and feel for their hair every day! If you take that approach, the sales will come naturally.

CH 1. DAILIES

Set yourself up for success from the start...

Awaken on your work day in plenty of time to get yourself ready and looking great. Eat a breakfast with protein so that you are nourished. Arrive 15-30 minutes ahead of your first scheduled client.

Front Desk Connect - Greet your front desk friend(s). Check your schedule. Get all of your client information for that day ready. Get a good feeling going for the clients you are servicing that day. Think about each client's HAIR as they arrive. What's your first impression of how it looks? What suggestions/compliments will you make?

Connect with your co-workers... Lightly.

Your greeting for each client... Let your eyes light up, with a big smile, even a hug if that's your style... Whatever your signature greeting style, be consistent with it and let your client feel SO VERY WELCOME! As you act this way, it's contagious! Again, just picture yourself at your doctor's office... How are you greeted? How would you LIKE to be greeted? It's the whole first impression rule... Even if you've done this client's hair for years, you likely haven't seen them for a month or more... they may be stressed, frazzled, feeling blue... YOU have the power to change how they FEEL by your greeting and how you welcome them... And surely by the time they leave the salon!

CH 2. YOUR APPEARANCE

Your appearance should ALWAYS be clean and fresh and fashionable. It has been said over and over again, to dress for the level of success that you want to attract... Try it!

Your "uniform" – why not make it easy on yourself and get a "work uniform" together that you like! It will make your mornings such a breeze when getting ready... Choose basic essentials. Black on bottom; black, grey, white on top. (Or any basic 2 or 3 colors on top). Makes coordinating and getting dressed for work so easy. You'll look polished and sleek every day.

IMPORTANT: Your hair should represent you. Make sure it looks terrific!

Wear stylish yet comfortable shoes with support. So essential.

CH 3. STATION APPEARANCE

At your salon station, there can be product overwhelm! Choose no more than 10 of your favorite finishing products – all that the client can purchase from your salon – and have them INSIDE your station to work with. For each client, have on your counter area ONLY those finishing products that you are choosing to use on their hair... Have a story about WHY you like the chosen products, why you are choosing them to use in THEIR hair, the desired results expected and examples... Put your other products, that you aren't choosing for their hair, AWAY into your station drawer or cupboard. This eliminates clutter and gets you thinking about what finishing products you will choose to use for each and every client.

As an EXAMPLE: "Gloria, before I blow your hair dry today, I am going to use a small amount of mousse at your root area right on top to build volume and lift from your scalp." Distribute and place the can of mousse right in her view. "Next I am going to add just 2 drops of this serum and distribute it through your hair and ends to give you a glossy feel and smooth blow out that will last into next week!" Distribute into her hair and place the serum right in her view.

Now you've educated her, and she sees what you just put into her hair. She is going to love the results. Of course she is going to want to leave the salon with both of those products to do her best to re-create the look again on her own. If you had just chatted away and put the products in without instructing her... and there were 10 other products cluttering up the space on your countertop, do you think she would even remember to ask what she should take home with her to re-create the finish you just crafted?

Do away with the clutter of finishing products at your station... De-clutter your countertop after EACH client, putting away products used and bringing out chosen products for your next client...

Be mindful, choose 1-2 of your favorite products for each result and stick with them. Create a story around them. Explain how using a particular product really changed your hair, or the look and feel of your client Debbie's hair... My client Deb mentioned that her hair was feeling dry. I asked what product she was using in her hair before blow drying. "Nothing," she replied. "I don't like my hair to feel heavy." "I understand," I answered, "I'd like you to try (product name). It's very light and provides the moisture and heat protection that your hair NEEDS." I added, "If your hands were feeling dry, would you put lotion on them? Think of your hair like you do your skin. Always needing moisture and protection – with different products from season to season." "Ah! Makes sense!" she said. I showed her how much of the product to use and how to distribute it into her hair before blow drying. What a difference! She loved the way her hair felt. A story helps to convey the value of purchasing and using the product you are recommending...

CH 4. FRONT DESK FRIENDS

The process...

From the start...

Calling for information, to book a hair appointment, walking in the front door, checking out...

How many times have you visited a doctor's office or called a doctor's office and not cared for the FRONT DESK STAFF?

First and foremost, make it a POINT to respect and appreciate your front desk staff person/s. This person/ staff member is your partner in your business, your partner in servicing your clients, and your partner in fulfilling your clients needs.

Let's call your front desk person Linda. Always greet Linda when you walk into the salon 15-30 minutes ahead of your first scheduled client. Take a look at your day's schedule and get a good feeling going for your day of clients ahead. Let Linda know that you return ALL calls by day's end if your clients have any questions or want to speak to you directly. Check your messages after your last client of the day. Let her know that you VALUE her role in accommodating your clients and always offer a 'cancellation list' for those wanting an appointment with you that day if you are already booked up. Let Linda know that you will find a way to accommodate your clients. Who knows, you may choose to stay late that day if you can… you can view this list and try your best to get your client scheduled in that day or soon after. Again – partner with her and let her know how much you appreciate her – she affects your client's experience on the phone and as they enter and exit the salon.

A coffee or unexpected treat for your front desk friend(s) from time to time can reinforce this too!

Front Desk Connect – Before leaving for the day, ALWAYS touch base with your front desk person(s) ALWAYS. Check your messages, next work day's schedule, and THANK THEM EVERY DAY before you leave. Remember, they are your front line on the phone, in person, etc…

Show them and tell them that you appreciate them. It will affect you.

CH 5. PRE-BOOK IMPORTANCE

At the end of each and every appointment, walk your client to the front desk... I know you are busy and your next client is likely waiting, but this is an important step to complete your client's visit. How many times have you been left in a doctor's room waiting and wondering... "Am I all done? Is he/she coming back in? I had one more question! Should I just go and check out?..." This step sets you apart from other stylists... From the greeting through the very end of their visit, you wrap it up with an offer of products to take home with them, and also to secure their next appointment at a time that works best for them.

1. "Would you like to take home the styling products that I used in your hair today?"

(Not, "do you need any products?" Can you hear the difference and the personal question?)

2. "Would you like (front desk friend name) to schedule your next visit?"

Add... "I want to make sure you get to return when it works best for you."

Then wrap it up with...

3. "Great! I can't wait to see you next time!" or "I can't wait to see you in 4 weeks!" ... You get the picture, make them feel that you are already looking forward to the next time you get to see them, visit with them and do their hair!

In between visits, since you have gathered their info. (e-mail address and cell phone number or other social media contact)... every so often, send them an e-mail regarding a trend or a picture that you think would look great for their hair and their style! Check in with them every once in a while to make sure they are having a great hair day or are easily styling their hair.

CH 6. GREAT ANSWERS TO CLIENT QUESTIONS & CONCERNS

Q. "How long have you been doing hair?"

If you're a seasoned hairdresser with 5 or more years of in-salon experience, go ahead and give your quick 'journey into hairdressing and where you have worked and trained as a stylist' answer. Condense your answer. Practice it. Make it sound juicy. You'll be asked this question more than once. Here's an example, "Oh, I have wanted to do hair ever since I felt the power of a great hair day! I have studied and trained with the best. I have loved doing hair for the past 12 years!"

If you're a new stylist, and it's evident that you're young, your answer could be, "I have loved styling hair all of my life – I'm new to this salon, but I have over 10 years of experience doing all of my friends hair in high school and my family's hair since I could pick up a brush!"

Q. "What's new and trendy in hair?"

Remember, you are the hair source for your clients... Pick one or two hair trends that you see on television, on celebrities, etc. right now and have it roll right off your tongue as an answer. "I am seeing a lot of darker hues in hair color trending right now – purples, violet blues, ..." (name a current actress or performer with the color). Talk about length, variation with bangs and fringe (name a well-known person wearing bangs). "And facial hair on men!" (cite a popular role model that is a male wearing facial hair and looking oh so good!). Be conscious of how those in the spotlight are wearing their hair. They are the trend-setters and you are the source.

Q. "How much? I just can't afford it..."

For a Hair Service:

Aaaah yes... There are clients out there that don't think a hair cut or service should cost so much. As much as you would like to answer with, "You get what you pay for", a much nicer 'more to educate them' answer might be: "Oh I know, I wish we didn't need to charge as much ... but if you factor in the years of education and time and skill investment along with our salon owner's overhead of rent, heat/cooling, insurances, product costs and staffing, not to mention water bill! - It's a bargain, really!"

For Hair product/s:

Professional products make all the difference. Seriously. Let your client know that it's like the cake without the icing. If they like cake with no icing, well... It really is just like baking. The prep your hair needs, the ingredients, and the finish. Like baking, without all of the steps, it won't turn out great. Most hair textures NEED products (fine/

limp, dry/coarse, curly) to provide the base or foundation for the blow-out and style. And to finish; products for hold, definition and shine are essential if you want your hair to feel great and look great all day long.

Q. "Am I too old for... Long hair? Coloring my hair?"

"Absolutley not!"... "As long as your hair looks and feels healthy and is easy for you to manage. Look at Maria Shriver and Goldie Hawn – both in their 60's – with long hair and looking ever so glamorous!"

"Absolutely not!"... "Coloring your hair gives it shine and vibrancy. And your hair color's tone compliments your skin." I often think of an attractive gray-haired actress and have my client picture them with their gray hair and then with golden blonde hair... Which do they find more attractive and youthful looking?... Always the golden blonde hair...

Always talk...

"What I am seeing..." You're the hair expert!

CH 7. THE HAIR DOCTOR

Think about it... You could very easily be your client's #1 service provider...

The one he or she sees the most often for personal service...

How often do you go to your doctor? Your dentist? Surely not every 4 weeks? Or 8-10 weeks? Especially not over the course of many years...

Of all service providers, a person's hairdresser is likely to be the one they visit the most often...

Second might be their doctor. And how do you feel when you visit your doctor?

From the time you walk in... Do you feel that you are greeted and attended to well? Do you feel that you have to wait long? Do you feel valued as a patient? That your doctor is genuinely glad to see you? Do you feel that you are listened to? Given the full attention you would like? A plan? Instructions?

Does your doctor ever check-in or follow-up with you to see how you are doing or feeling?

Do you feel rushed?

... Put yourself in the place of a patient seeing their doctor... transfer that to a client seeing their hairdresser.

WIN them over. KEEP them returning for LIFE!

CH 8. CLIENT FOCUS

The focus must be on THEM...the CLIENT.

But again, no matter how brilliantly trained, or how much education, or what salon you work in,

WHERE DO YOU LEARN HOW TO HANDLE PEOPLE??

Not only do clients LOOK better and refreshed when they leave your chair,

They FEEL so much better, sometimes for getting whatever was bothering them off of their chest... Even just being "listened to" makes them feel good.

We are in charge of making them look and feel good. No one else has this role...

"Free Therapy" and "Free Listening,"

Conversation Skills = Customer Retention,

HAIR... It's one of the 1st things people notice about you...

YOUR HAIR... It's one of the biggest ways that we show our identity to other people.

Focus on your client. From start to finish. Listen. Keep the conversation POSITIVE. Always. They will feel your attention and your focus on them. And they will FEEL GOOD.

CH 9. MALE CLIENTS

All applies...

Make them feel so welcome and listened to and always offer them change...

Remember to educate them too... On hair cuts, what's trending right now, how to use products... I often have my male clients put the product in their hands, so that I can show them how much product I suggest they use for the look that they want to achieve... I show them the right amount to use for their hair type... I then, with clean hands without product in, show them how to distribute the product into their hair, and then have THEM follow... just after I have showed them. Often times they do a great job, or at times they need a bit more direction on how to work it and finish the look... They will remember this way, having done it themselves.

ALWAYS hand your client a dampened towel afterward to wipe their hands of any product... nice extra touch...

With trends, keep an eye on detail in men's cuts and looks...

Side burns, for example... are they long or short, skinny or following the natural hair growth, etc...

Products... what's in? What's needed to create the look and finish for their great hair cut? Always introduce them to the product that you are using to finish their hair with at your station, and why it is your product of choice for their hair. If they have been using a shiny gel for years and a matte textured look is in, suggest they shelf their gel for now and show them how to get a great look with a hair paste.

Emphasize the NEED for them to use a finishing product in their hair. You have just given them a terrific hair cut. Without product in their hair to finish their look, their hair can't look great! I often tell my male clients that without product, their hair will resemble a Q-tip. Fuzzy and soft. Not their best look. It makes the biggest difference – air-dried hair or hair with the right finishing product in it... Bradley Cooper and Leonardo DiCaprio don't get that look without finishing product in their hair!

Color... Do they have any gray hair? Is it time to blend? Educate them on their options...

CH 10. REPEAT BUSINESS

DO THE MATH... (just as an example: 200 clients + 4 days a week with 8-12 clients per day = $$)

How many REGULAR CLIENTS, or HAIR CLIENTS FOR LIFE, do you want? 100? 200? 300?

Regular clients (HAIR CLIENTS FOR LIFE!) = Regularly Booked Schedule = Regular Income = Circle of Great Clients!

It's up to you... How many days/hours do you want to work each week? How many clients would you like to service each day? How much money do you want to make? Mock it up... Do the math... There is your goal!

Now, make your clients find you special enough, because you have made them feel special enough, to come back EACH hair visit and stay with you for the long run.

It is so much better, so much more interesting, and so much more dependable to know who your clients are and that you have a regular stream of these steady clients each and every week.

Let's say that you have 250 clients that you consistently service... I understand that some are your "bread & butter" clients, every 4 weeks in for a root touch-up with highlights/lowlights every so often. A glossing, a haircut, possible waxing service. Clients and their needs vary, which will vary the time and services you provide them and the time and money that they spend with you.

Never push extra services to your client unless their hair will absolutely benefit. Clients can smell a sales person trying to up their tab. If you remain honest, skilled, offer them change and treat them like you would a good friend, they will trust you. If you find that their hair would benefit from an extra service from time to time, offer and explain why. They will almost always accept.

Every day is varied and interesting! That's what makes our work as hairdressers so great! And creative!

CH 11. THE ART OF LISTENING...

LISTEN...

Shhhhhhhhhh......

ZIP IT!

Concentrate on your breathing... Do you know that most people shallow breathe all day long? Take a deep breath right now. Fill your lungs with fresh air. Fill them up deep. Exhale. Feel the release. 5 deep breaths will re-oxygenate your lungs and your brain. While your client is talking..., do not jump in to talk... Breathe... Concentrate and rejuvenate yourself!

Make sure you are talking much less than your client about anything other than HAIR. Personal, chatty light conversation is fine, but let them do most of the talking following your questions...

And as they answer, zip it. Listen... It's their time to share when they are talking... Not yours... Now breathe...

CH 12. STRUGGLING FOR CONVERSATION

When you're struggling for conversation with a client, always ask them a question about their hair...

"How are most of your friends wearing their hair?"

"How are most of those in your office wearing their hair?"

Not to get them to wear their hair like the status quo, but it will start a conversation about their hair and how those around them are wearing their hair...

Talk about trends – what you're seeing...

Ask "Have you ever played with hot rollers, velcro rollers, texture spray, beach wave spray, ...?"

"Do you ever wear your hair up? Pony tail it? Wear head bands? Braid it?"

If you really CARE about your clients, they feel it. They will trust you. Openly engage.....

Asking them questions about their HAIR will always spark conversation.

CH 13. HAIR PICTURES

Your client arrives, with a picture of how they would like their hair to look, on their phone or tablet or torn out of a magazine...

Before you think to yourself "Yah great, and you probably want to look just like Rhianna too!..." STOP... Take a look at the photo, and then look at your client.

Is it a fit? Do they have the same hair type/texture as far as you can tell from the picture?

Your immediate response should be "I LOVE PICTURES! WORKING FROM A VISUAL IS GREAT!" That has always been my go-to line... it immediately makes your client feel comfortable and instills their confidence in you.

Have the client let you know WHAT they like about the hair in the picture... Ask some detective questions. Do they like the overall color? The dimensional color? If your client has brought in a picture of a hair color they would like, have them hold the picture up to the side of their own face and look into the mirror... Do they like it against their own skin tone? Do they like it, maybe a shade lighter? So many times when I have had the client hold the picture up next to their own face, they say "Oh that's too dark. I like it. But maybe a bit lighter?" You have just saved yourself from a color correction. So often the model in the picture has a different skin tone, or the lighting for the photograph is a factor. If the color is quite different from what your client is wearing right now... suggest that you go darker with their color "in stages" by choosing a darker color that is a level or two lighter than the one in the picture; or by adding depth with lowlights to start, as opposed to taking the whole overall color darker in one step... They will thank you. And if you both decide you like the outcome, you can go a shade darker or add more lowlights during their next visit!

At times, the desired hair color or cut won't turn out exactly like the picture ...

Let them know that with hair color, it's a process. Often you can match the desired results on the first visit if that was the plan. Other times it may take a few visits to build the color according to what their color is to begin with, the shape and porosity of their hair, how their hair accepts color, etc. There are several factors involved and once you have worked with their hair a few times, you will get to know its texture and how it accepts color.

As for a desired hair cut/look from a picture, let your client know if that look is achievable with their own hair type and texture. Does the picture show the hair with a flat ironed finish, loose curled finish, volume? Educate them on the techniques they will need to do and learn, to create that finished look.

What these questions and the discussion will give your client is the feeling that "my stylist understands my hair!" which also equals "my stylist is a great listener!"

CH 14. HAIR CHALLENGES

Do your research. Thanks to the Internet, it can be so quick and easy! New products and solutions are at our fingertips... if you have a client with thinning hair challenges, research for them:

Thinning hair solutions for men

Thinning hair solutions for women

Hair regenerative products

Hair replacement options

Hair enhancement solutions

Product lines

Natural approaches – Vitamins

Essential Oils

BE THEIR RESOURCE

HAIR CHANGES in your HAIR CLIENTS FOR LIFE:

Many things can cause your client's hair to change:

Illness

Surgery

Aging

Scalp condition

Notice, and let them know you care. Offer suggestions and solutions:

Some examples include vitamins and supplements they can try, and also products in your salon that apply.

Research the most natural hair color lines for clients with skin sensitivities. Also take the extra step to protect the skin around their ears and hairline when applying their hair color.

Research and suggest. Let your client know that you're going to do some research for them and then offer them some choice solutions. They will appreciate this extra effort and personal attention.

CH 15. SLOW-DAYS...

The whole idea is not to sound like you have a slow day or open space in your day.

Ideas...

E-mail or text and offer to targeted clients:

"Our salon is offering half-off highlights today! Letting my favorite blonde clients know! Call/text and I'll fit you in!"

Or... "Free glossing treatment with hair cuts today! Call/text and I'll fit you in!"

Or... "Just got out of a class and learned a new color technique... Can you make it in today? The model made me think of you and your hair!"

Or... "Our salon is offering 25% off today! Call and I will do my best to schedule you in!"

Or... "Just had a cancellation today – want in?"

Think of ways to offer excitement, and an opportunity to treat themselves and to jump at that opportunity. With today's flexible work schedules and people's life schedules... often your clients can make it happen, when they would normally be thinking that you are surely booked.

Another good one, "Half-off blow-outs today!" ...

Ideas... Opportunities...

In today's techno-electronic times that we live and work in, I hope that you have ALL of your clients' cell phone numbers and e-mail addresses. If not, get busy and get them... Even if you're "old school" like me and keep a giant index card box full of client formulas, notes, etc., make sure that you have up-to-date cell phone numbers and e-mail addresses for all of your clients. It's a great way to keep in touch with your clients especially on a "slow day"... you can reach out to a select few that you know have a flexible schedule, or may be due to come in, etc...

It's also great to e-mail all of your clients with incentives, specials, etc... E-mail blasts can also keep you in your clients minds by sending out seasonal hair tips for keeping their hair looking and feeling FANTASTIC!

Become their HAIR SOURCE...

Another great way to fill your "slow day" is to fill yourself up with education. Grab your phone or tablet and educate yourself on hair techniques and personal communication skills.

Client inventory is another great use of your time on a slow day... going through your list of clients, really giving thought to their hair and what you can suggest for them to make it look and feel amazing. Make notes... The next time you get to see them, let them know that you were thinking about them and their hair, and that you have a suggestion or a new product that you want them to try or a new way of layering or coloring or texturizing their hair... They will feel special.

CH 16. HOW TO LET GO OF (FIRE!) A CLIENT GRACEFULLY...

Certain clients are, well..., an ENERGY SUCK...
KNOW that you can let them go.

NEW PEOPLE, NEW ENERGY, WILL FILL THE GAP.

PROMISE.

Sometimes you just need to clear the energy after you've serviced a client... Do you sometimes feel like a client's energy is still clinging to you after they have left your chair or space? That they have sucked you dry? Some clients are "energy vampires"... If you have one, or several, there are some simple exercises that can help you "protect yourself" from their energy, and "clear" their energy after they have gone...

Here is one that I use: before this client arrives, picture yourself enveloped in a bubble of your favorite color... this bubble protects you from that client's energy drain!

If the client has left and you feel wiped out, take a moment to head to the bathroom where you'll have a minute of privacy. Place your arms above your head, next sweep them down to your sides and back up again, in an angel wings motion, saying in your head that you have just cleared all energy attached to you and are now refreshed... I do this. It works!

But what if you really don't want to service them any longer as a client? Well, there is never an easy way, and I know they are a paying client, but if they are just draining your energy, or are never happy, or are always calling to have you "fix something" and you just DREAD when you see their name in your day's schedule... they aren't a good fit as a HAIR CLIENT FOR LIFE for you...

To dance around it or hope they change isn't your solution. Be honest and bite the bullet...

Call them or send them an email to let them know that you are releasing them as a client at this time, and are referring them to another stylist that you believe will be a better fit for them. Take the heat. Let them know that you feel you just aren't hitting the mark with their hair and know that a change will benefit them... If they go on and on, and want to stay as your client, be firm and let them know that a change will be great! (For YOU!!). Keep your tone positive yet firm. You are the one in control, and trust me, you will feel 100% better and feel a big weight lift off of your shoulders once you've done it.

An example:

"(Client name), I just feel that I am not meeting your hair needs. I am referring you to (name) in our salon who has fresh energy and ideas and I believe will be a better fit for your hair goals. (Let that stylist know the background. She/he may welcome the challenge!)

Let your front desk staff know the situation and who to schedule this client with instead of you. The energy match with a different stylist (or even a different salon) will be all for the best.

We are all different and it just isn't worth the stress if you have a client that is continually draining your energy. Trust me, a new client will fill that space for you. YOU WON'T REGRET IT. SO WORTH IT.

CH 17. FINDING THE BEST SALON/ WORK ENVIRONMENT FOR YOU

As a new hairdresser...

Ask yourself, what kind of salon environment will best support you and your growth as a hairdresser? Are you attracted to a big salon environment with lots of stylists and clients? A medium sized salon environment? Or a smaller, boutique-like or studio-like feel with only a few stations that tends to be more quiet? Walk in to a salon that you feel may be a good fit. Browse their retail products. How do you like the feel of the environment? If you like it, ask the front desk person if they are hiring and if there is a mentoring or assistant program offered where you can begin by learning alongside a seasoned hairdresser. It's best to "shadow" for a day or even a half-day to get the feel of a salon, the flow of the energy there, the clients, your fellow hairdressers, etc. You'll get a good idea by spending some time there on a typical day. Trust your instincts. It needs to feel right for you.

As a skilled, seasoned hairdresser…

Ask yourself, have you outgrown your current work location? Do you need to head to a more quiet place? Or do you need to adjust your work schedule to create the change you need? Sometimes you just need to step away on a vacation or walk into a different salon in your area "to buy some hair spray" to get a feel of a different vibe. It will often reinforce that you are just where you need to be. Your current work environment is great, you just need to take care of YOU and make sure that you are not heading for burn out.

Or if you do find that you need a change, ask yourself what isn't working for you at your current location… Do you need to adjust your hours? Or adjust the days that you work? You don't want to be a salon jumper, it's not a good way to build and maintain client consistency. Ask yourself what your needs are to create the best work environment for yourself and then ask if you can work with your salon owner to create it. Open communication is always best. Salon drama and walk-outs rarely turn out well. The grass is hardly ever greener…

CH 18. BURN OUT

If you are feeling burned out, tired, in a rut, in a funk...

Schedule a full morning or a full evening or better yet – A FULL DAY OFF to yourself ASAP! Not to run errands or get things done around the house or meet with friends... A full day for YOURSELF. Get a good night's rest and in the morning, grab this book "HAIR CLIENTS FOR LIFE!", head to your favorite coffee shop, plunk down into the most comfy looking chair with a cappuccino (coffee is my favorite brain invigorator!) and re-visit...

WHY YOU ARE A HAIR STYLIST...

1.

2.

3.

WHAT CHANGES CAN YOU MAKE TO RE-FRESH YOUR DRIVE?

1.

2.

3.

LIST THINGS YOU CAN DO TO RE-FUEL YOURSELF:

1.

2.

3.

Staying fresh with education through your salon is essential for your career (BRAVO to salons offering continuing education and classes! Always take advantage of these. Even if you are a seasoned stylist. They re-motivate and you are bound to pick up a new technique or fresh trend to add to your skills).

Education on the Internet (trade sites such as behindthechair. com, YouTube, tutorials, etc.) ... is easy to access too!

But even more important is to educate and update your PERSONAL COMMUNICATION SKILLS and your PERSONAL GROWTH.

Internet search "personal growth" or "positive communication skills" and a wealth of information will be at your fingertips. With the connection of the Internet, you will come across great authors and speakers who have videos that you can view and listen to on YouTube (I often play these as I'm getting ready for my day in the morning) to inspire, lift you up, and re-energize you in a positive way! Authors Wayne Dyer and Louise Hay; and sites such as mindvalleyacademy.com and mindbodygreen.com, are just a few of my favorites.

RE-VISIT...

WHY
YOU
ARE
A HAIR
STYLIST

What changes can you make to refresh yourself and your FOCUS?

RE-VISIT...

Pick a day of the month... the first Monday of each month is often an easy way to remember, and take time this day to go through your list of clients...

Appreciate, reach out, re-visit what you're doing with their hair cut, color, and care... I find this is a good way to re-set my focus.

CH 19. SELF-CARE SUGGESTIONS:

YOU ARE NOT ONLY A HAIRDRESSER... YOU ARE A SPIN DOCTOR, A THERAPIST, AN ADVISOR, A BEAUTIFIER AND AN UPLIFTER...

BUT... to do this best, consistently and most effectively, for your Hair Clients for Life, you MUST be TAKING CARE OF YOU.

I feel these suggestions are essential:

MEDITATE – every morning. For 5-10 minutes. Sit, wrap your hands around your first morning cup of coffee or tea, and close your eyes. Focus on your breath. In and out. Deep breaths. If you find your mind wandering and focusing on the day's activities ahead, STOP. Re-focus your attention, and think about what makes you feel grateful. Next, just sit in silence for 1 minute. Finish your coffee or tea. And stretch. OK, now begin your morning..... This simple, 5 minute exercise changed my life. Seriously. If you take a moment to quiet your mind at the start of your day and set your intentions for the day ahead; it's amazing how calm and clear-headed you can begin your day.

WATER – essential for brain function, which you will need with a busy day filled with your favorite clients. It is suggested to take your body weight, divide that number in half, which is the amount of ounces you should drink throughout your day to keep well hydrated. Drink water throughout your day – use a favorite glass water bottle to hydrate and keep your brain fresh. I use a glass water bottle that I squeeze a fresh lemon or lime in to flavor my water and once it's empty, I refill with fresh water. If it is in front of you, on your work station, every day, it will become a habit for you to stay well hydrated. What a difference it makes to keep a steady stream of water nourishing your brain as you work! Nourish yourself first, to best support and service your clients. Try it. Make it a habit. Another game changer.

FOOD – eat every 3-4 hours, ideally. Snacking and grazing is best with a long day of clients. It will keep your blood sugar steady, your energy even, and your body feeling good. Best is a balance of lean protein, fruits and vegetables. Heavy foods or fried foods are sure to get you feeling sluggish. Try and make clean, fresh eating a habit. You will feel and look amazing.

EXERCISE – as hairdressers, we feel like we work out every day! We're on our feet, we are bending, stretching, blow drying, walking all over the salon... But it's still important to do something to nourish yourself with exercise when you are not in the salon. Stretch at night when you get home. Even 10 minutes of stretching after a long day at the salon will do your body wonders before bed. Practice yoga, power walk, get outdoors when the weather is nice. Make it something you enjoy and you are likely to stick with it and notice the benefits!

BREAK – BREATHE – RE-FUEL – Always take a break in your day to breathe and re-fuel.

Do not "squeeze in a client" and rob yourself of your lunch break during a 10 hour work day... stay late and take them at the end of your day if possible, but never skip your lunch and moment to nourish yourself to squeeze in a client that doesn't have an appointment. Seriously, it will domino the rest of your day and affect not only YOU, but all of your clients you have yet to greet and service.

$$ - It's not all about the money. Yes, you work to earn money and make a living, but you also want to enjoy your work, keep yourself healthy and nourished and balanced with good energy. If you cram too many people into your day, and get caught in a negative thought cycle... you'll "PAY" greatly.

BOUNDARIES – set them. You will feel stronger and more empowered. Always saying YES does not make you a better hairdresser, it makes you a push-over.

Know your worth... Raise your prices a bit if you're feeling it... Even adding $ to every chemical service will impact your weekly total. And you're definitely worth it.

CH 20. THE POWER OF POSITIVITY

"Positive Feed" – Feed yourself consistently with positive thoughts and information.

Positivity – Energy – It's contagious! We all like to be around people who are positive and have good energy. Reading self-help books, motivational books, philosophers notes, YouTube videos on the power of positive thinking... there is so much available... anything to get positive feed into your mind is good. I input positive information into my head every day. Forego the news and listen to a podcast or webinar on positive thinking instead. It will impact you greatly and become contagious as a habit.

Connect with your client about their HAIR, and connect with your client PERSONALLY... Keeping all of your interaction with them POSITIVE.

POSITIVE 1st impressions – Keep an open mind, just as you would want someone to have of you.

ATTITUDE - Have an attitude of gratitude ... 5 things... focus on 5 things you are grateful for as soon as you awaken each morning, and just before you fall asleep.

And throughout the day, keep your thoughts on what you are thankful for, always in your mind.

BREATHE - While you are shampooing or blow drying, always make sure you are getting in some deep breaths. It will re-energize you if you're feeling tired, and it will de-stress you if you are running behind schedule... 5... Deep...Breaths...

APPRECIATION - Make your clients feel valued and appreciated.... Thank you notes and texts, a bowl of wrapped mints at your station, keep a small basket of sample products that you can offer ...

GIFTS - At holiday time, offer travel hair products wrapped in a cellophane bag with candies as a treat to lift their spirits and make them feel special. Buy in bulk – wrap and begin to give away December 1st... Keep in a big basket on your station! Make it festive and creative!

Positive....

Mirror...

Even if YOU aren't feeling great, are having trouble in a relationship, are feeling stressed out... about anything!... ACT AS IF ALL IS WELL...Look in that mirror, ACT AS IF... and watch what happens. Things will begin to shift in a positive way!

Talk positive.

Always give positive answers and feedback to your clients.

Always keep the conversation positive, uplifting, focused on THEM, their hair needs 1st and foremost.

CH 21. THE SPIRITUAL SIDE OF HAIRDRESSSING

Remember, and know, that every day, you are serving others:

As a Healer,

An Uplifter,

A Hair Doctor...

You have chosen this profession to serve people and help them to LOOK and FEEL fantastic!

You affect their day in such a positive way.

You change the way they look and feel about themselves.

You touch their hair, and their hair has a profound effect on them. It's their first impression to others, and it's what they see first in the mirror.

In the spiritual realm, the head is often referred to as the "Halo" or "Crown Chakra"; and as you shampoo, comb through, style and shape your client's hair, you have such an opportunity to positively affect them. Even heal them... of their stress, headache, etc.

Many new clients are anxious coming in to a salon to have their hair done. They are trusting that you will listen and provide a great service. They want to walk out of your care really loving their hair and feeling great!

It takes skill to connect with clients and earn their trust. Once you do, they are comfortable and won't want to go through the anxiety of finding a new hairdresser.

It's so important to earn their trust and win them over as a client for life, and to re-connect with each and every one of them to KEEP them as HAIR CLIENTS FOR LIFE!

Be mindful, each and every day. How can you best serve your clients? How can you make their day? How can you make their visit with you extra special? How can you help them to feel fantastic!?

You're not "just doing hair," you are a professional hairdresser servicing your clientele of HAIR CLIENTS FOR LIFE as your career soars!

Watch your mind talk... Your inner chatter... Make sure it's positive and supportive of your clients... and first, and foremost, of YOURSELF.

If you take care of yourself first, you will naturally, through your service, take care of others.

Get good rest. 7-8 hours each night.

Eat real food – plenty of fresh fruits, vegetables, lean protein. Eat often, in small portions to keep your blood sugar and energy steady. (This can change your inner world, your health, and your energy!)

Hydrate all day long with water.

Meditate each morning (and evening too!)... Start with just 5 minutes. I started with my first morning cup of coffee. Instead of carrying it around the house with me while I started laundry and made beds, I would make that fresh cup of coffee and find a quiet spot to sit, sipping it while it was still warm, and counting my blessings, giving thanks inside of my head for all that was going well in my life and for those that I love and care for. Set your intention for the day. Make it positive and self-healing. At night, light a candle and count 5 blessings. Meditation can be this simple.

Do not jam pack your day. A "no space" day will get you stressed and eventually sick, and then you'll need all kinds of "space" to get well. Busy days can be great, but jam-packed days are just not healthy. You must drink water, eat, take bathroom breaks, stretch and catch your breath. You are a creative hairdresser. Not a machine.

Set boundaries around your schedule and stick to them. You are worth it.

Create space... Move your body with a few stretches, toe touches, twists. Drink some lemon water or green tea.

If you can walk outside for a few minutes in between clients or while your client's hair is processing to get a different view and breathe in some fresh air to re-charge for a moment – that will benefit you, too!

Remember, you are an amazing hairdresser, with the skills to change the appearance of your clients, affecting not only how they look, but how they FEEL.

You're an up-lifter! A hair god or goddess! What an awesome job you have!

CONCLUSION

ABOVE ALL... CREATE AN EXPERIENCE FOR YOUR CLIENT...

When they are there in the salon for their hair service, do they feel cared for? Have you given them a consultation every time? Sometimes a consultation will be a minute, other visits the consult may last longer if you have a suggestion or different direction to take their hair... Do they feel listened to? Throughout their time with you, were they serviced with great looking hair to look and feel their very best?

ONE LAST RE-CAP...
START TO FINISH:
GREET – CONSULT – SHAMPOO & CONDITION –
SERVICE – TEND-TO – TALK & EDUCATE – FINISH –
OFFER PRODUCTS & PRE-BOOK – END VISIT

HOW DID YOUR CLIENT FEEL WHEN THEY LEFT YOUR CARE?

GORGEOUS? UPLIFTED? THEY'LL BE BACK TIME AND TIME AGAIN...

IN FACT, THEY WILL BE YOUR HAIR CLIENT FOR LIFE!!

CONNECT:

www.julieholler.com

Printed in the United States
By Bookmasters